Rethinking Church
Community called out to take responsibility

The M-series is a collection of short, accessible papers and articles from Micah Global, being developed in response to the need for clear, authoritative statements on key themes. They form a foundation of historical and current ideas that contribute to our understanding and practice of integral mission. They aim to promote reflection, dialogue, articulation and action on the major concepts and issues that move us towards transforming mission.

The M-series is an essential resource for practitioners, theologians, students, leaders, and teachers.

M-Series from im:press

Titles in print:
Integral Mission: Biblical Foundations
by Melba Maggay

The Five Marks of Mission:
Making God's Mission Ours
by Chris Wright

Towards Transformed Honour
by Arley Loewen

Living in God's Story:
Understanding the Bible's Grand Narrative
by Mark Galpin

Corruption and the Church:
A Brief Introduction
by Martin Allaby

Rethinking Church
Community called out
to take responsibility

Johannes Reimer
With Christopher Wright

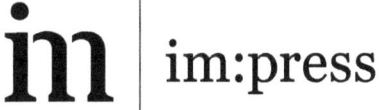

Copyright © Johannes Reimer
The author asserts the moral right to be identified as the author of this work

Published by im:press An imprint of Micah Global

ISBN: 978-1-4855-0009-4

All rights reserved.
No part of this book may be transmitted or reproduced in any form or by any means, including but not restricted to photocopying, recording, or by any information storage and retrieval system, without written permission from the publisher; except for brief quotations in printed reviews.

Printed and bound by Ingram Spark

Contents

Foreword	7
Contributions	8
Historic Reality in Contextual Diversity	10
Images of the Church	12
What does the Old Testament Say?	13
What does the New Testament Say?	21
Master Images of the Church	22
The People of God – a Matrix of Life	24
A Temple of the Spirit – A Place to meet God	28
Body of Christ – The Fullness of Competence	31
Other Images of the Church in the New Testament	32
Missionary by Nature	48
Christ Incarnate	49
The Church Incarnate	50
All for All	52
Mission with the People	54
Gifted, trained and sent	55
Sign and messenger of the Kingdom	58
Bibliography	60

Foreword

Over the years of facilitating integral mission conversations and dialogues around God's mission, a question keeps arising – "What do we mean by church?" There seems to be a growing need to explore this question and seek a way of answering it in a way that unites us for God's mission.

Micah invited Johannes Reimer to lead a working group on this question and it soon became apparent that instead of asking the question "What is church?" we needed to radically rethink church by exploring God's Word together and drawing out key attributes that we could all agree on.

For grassroots transformation to take place we need grassroots agents of change – who better that God's people called out to take responsibility for God's world?

Micah saw the need to define Church in terms that are applicable in different contexts and cultures around the world. As an interdenominational network we intentionally do not promote certain denominational accents or perspectives. This does not mean that we do not recognise the validity of such accents or perspectives; rather we seek to promote a Biblical vision of the Missional Church. In so doing we realise that we will need the courage for change to rethink church through an integral mission lens.

This M.Series booklet is the culmination of this reflection and we are excited to see the ongoing dialogue that leads to God's church being equipped and inspired to be all that she has been called to be.

We invite each reader to prayerfully and courageously engage with this reflection for the sake of God's Mission.

Contributions

Rethinking Church was initially birthed out of the Micah Global Consultation in Peru in 2015 where the need to rethink our understanding of church was raised. It was agreed to set up a working group to address this, chaired by Johannes Reimer. The initial drafts of the subsequent Micah Paper written by Johannes Reimer were sent to the Micah Panel of Reference and interest members who had expressed a desire to be a part of this process. Their contributions and feedback have greatly enriched the paper. In particular we want to thank Chris Wright for his input in the Old Testament and corresponding New Testament links on understanding church; Deborah Hancox and Sergej Kiel for their editing and input, and Tearfund UK (Hannah Swithinbank and her team) for their helpful feedback. Based on this interest and expressed need to share the collated learning, the team drew out the core reflections from the Micah Paper and developed it into an M.Series booklet. This is the result of this inspiring collaboration, with the overarching input from Johannes Reimer.

The concept of a **Micah Paper** is drawn from two types of publications:

White Paper: the purpose of a white paper is to help readers understand an issue, solve a problem, or make a decision. Types of white papers include:

- A **policy document** often produced by governments that sets out their proposals for future legislation and/or strategy. They can be published as authoritative papers that may contain a draft bill that is being planned. The paper provides a basis for further consultation, discussions and actions.

- A **guiding document** that informs readers in a concise manner about a complex issue and presents the issuing body's philosophy on the matter.

- An **informational document** to promote or highlight the features of a solution, a product or a service.

Encyclical Letter: the purpose of the circular letter is to inform churches about issues of concern and guide them in their response.

- A **letter** sent out by the Pope to inform Bishops and the wider church (and even the public), in which he lays down policy on religious, moral, or political issues.

- A **doctrinal and/or theological reflection** to draw on to inform action.

Every generation faces challenges in their context and should be prompted to reflect with fresh perspectives, both theological and practically, drawing on past learning and at the same time, renewing perspectives, with an openness for new insights and transformational shifts. Micah Papers seek to enable this reflection and encourage a Spirit-led response to the issues of concern faced by our generation.

Purpose: Micah Papers should be seen as a consultative tool to enable development of reflective thinking and holistic action. They should play a dual role in presenting integral mission perspectives, as well as inviting further opinions and discussions on the issues presented.

Historic Reality in Contextual Diversity

Wherever the Christian faith has found its way into hearts, minds and cultures of people, churches have been formed. Churchless Christianity does not exist.

But what do we mean by Church?

Martin Luther confidently writes in his famous Smalcald[1] 'Articles': *"Thank God, a seven-year-old child knows what the church is, namely holy believers and sheep who hear the voice of their Shepherd."* However, believers seldom agree on what church is, and the question "What do we mean by church?" seems to come up in many discussions.

Views on the Church and understanding of the meaning of the word have evolved over generations, influenced by different political and cultural contexts, at times manipulated by ambitious church leaders, and directed by biased theological positions.

It is therefore no surprise that we face major divisions among Christians as to what church actually is.

---

1 Luther 1537: Smalcald Articles (III, XII).

Since the Reformation, more than 40 thousand denominations have developed over the years.

There are even more ecclesial forms.

Many claim exclusively to know the 'proper' understanding of what the Church of Christ is and what her mission and task encompasses.

This booklet seeks to find a common denominator for a Biblical understanding of the Church.

Images of the Church

WHAT church is must be defined by God's revelation. Though we may vary on the different ways God reveals truth to us, the common denominator for us all is that God's revelation is given in the Bible. Scripture is therefore the foundation of our Christian theology and theological practice. Every other view and perspective must submit to the authority of Scripture.

> Proper ecclesiology is Biblical ecclesiology.

Most Christian traditions agree on this, so why all the divisions and disagreements?

The Bible does not offer us a concise and unified description and vision of what the Church is.

This was the conclusion of the Swiss theologian Eduard Schweizer[2], who conducted a prominent study on the Church in the New Testament, a finding that many accept. It is important, however, to add that Schweizer, stating this conclusion, still believed that there can be no other foundation of the Church beside the New Testament[3]. However, we would add 'beside the Bible', as New Testament images are rooted in the Old Testament, and in order to establish a truly Biblical theology of the Church, it is important to demonstrate both the Old and New Testament synergies.

---

2 Schweizer 1959:7.
3 Ibid.

What does the Old Testament Say?[4]

The Roots of Church in the Old Testament

If we think of the Church as the community of people who confess Jesus of Nazareth as Lord and Saviour, and who seek to live as his followers in the power of the Holy Spirit, then the historical origin of that community, defined in relation to Jesus Christ, must be traced back to the day of Pentecost in New Testament. However, Christians believe that the Church is a community that has been called into existence by God, a people constituted by God for God's own purpose in the world. And the roots of that calling and constitution go much further back than Pentecost. If we want to understand what happened in the Gospel and Acts, we have to set this New Testament story in the light of Israel in the Old Testament. That means going back to Abraham. But then we discover that we can't understand Abraham either, unless we set him in the context of all that happened before him. So all in all, it is best to start at the very beginning – not with the birth of the Church, but with the birth of the world. We need to look briefly at Genesis 1-11.

The Bible begins with the story of creation. The universe we inhabit is the creation of the one, living, personal God, who made it 'good'. He created us in his own image, to rule over the earth on his behalf, with spiritual and moral responsibilities: to love and obey God, to love and serve one another, and to enjoy and care for the rest of creation. However, with the entrance of sin and evil into human life, all of these dimensions of our existence have been fractured and distorted. We chose to rebel against our creator, and substitute our own moral autonomy for his authority. We live with all manner of personal and social sin – fear, anger, violence, injustice, oppression and corruption. And we exploit, pollute and destroy the earth God told us to care for. The climax

[4] Reflections from Old Testament by Dr Christopher Wright

of this sad catalogue of human sin comes with the story of the tower of Babel in Genesis 11. To prevent unified humanity acting in total arrogance, God divided human languages with the resultant confusion of communication. By the end of this part of the biblical story, we find a humanity that is fractured, divided, and scattered over the face of the earth that is under God's curse. Is there any hope for the world – specifically for the nations of humanity?

God's answer to the question posed by Genesis 1-11 is the story contained in the rest of the Bible, from Genesis 12 to Revelation 22. It is the story of God's work of redemption within history. It centres on the cross and resurrection of Jesus Christ. And it comes to its climactic finale in the return of Christ and his reign over the new creation. The remarkable thing is that this whole Bible story begins and ends with the nations of humanity. In Genesis 11 they were united in arrogance, only to be scattered under judgement. In Revelation 7:9 they will be gathered as 'a great multitude that no-one could count, from every nation, tribe, people and language.' This final picture of the nations in Revelation, however, is actually a portrait of the Church – the multinational community of God's redeemed humanity. And its multinational nature goes back to the promise God made to Abraham, that through him all nations on earth would be blessed. (Gen. 12:3)

So the Church, considered as the community of God's people throughout history, fills the gap between Babel and the new creation. This is the community that begins with one man and his wife (Abraham and Sarah), becomes a family, then a nation, and then a vast throng from every nation and language. This is the church in its fully biblical perspective.

What can we learn about this community from the account of its earliest beginning in the call of Abraham? Three things stand out in the promises and narrative of Genesis, three things that should be essential marks of the people of God in any era: blessing, faith and obedience.

A community of blessing

Blessing was God's first word, as he successively blessed his own acts of creation in Genesis 1. After the flood, God blessed Noah and made a covenant with all life on earth. But repeated sin and failure seemed to reinforce only the language and reality of God's curse. Where can blessing be found? God's answer is to call Abraham and to promise to bless him and his descendants. So this new community stemming from Abraham will be the recipients of God's blessing. There is a fresh start here, for humanity and creation. But blessing is not just passively received. Abraham is also mandated to 'be a blessing' (Gen. 12:2). The covenant promise God makes to him is that all nations on earth will find blessing through him. It takes the rest of the Bible to show how this can be fulfilled, but it does mark out this community as those who both experience God's blessing and are the means of passing it on to others. Blessing received and blessing shared, is part of the essence of the Church.

A community of faith

'Abraham believed God, and it was credited to him as righteousness,' says Paul (Galatians 3:6), echoing Genesis 15:6. Hebrews also strongly highlights Abraham as a man of faith (Hebrews 11:8-19), having earlier said that *'without faith it is impossible to please God.'* So the community that stems from Abraham must be marked as a people who trust in the promise of God, rather than trusting in their capacity to build their own future security (as they tried at Babel). This is why one common name for Christians is particularly appropriate – they are simply *'believers'*.

A community of obedience

Because of his faith, Abraham obeyed God; he got up and left his homeland at God's command. And when he faced the supreme test of sacrificing the son who embodied all God had promised him, he was willing to obey even then, though God intervened to stop him. At the climax of that narrative, God re-confirms his promise to bless all nations because of Abraham's obedience (Genesis 22:15-18). Hebrews 11 and James 2:20-24 set Abraham's obedience alongside his faith as proof of his authentic relationship with God.

The Church, then, in tracing its roots back to God's call and promise to Abraham, finds some of its key identity marks, with more to follow later. It is the community that not only experiences God's rich blessing but is also commissioned to be the means of blessing to others. It is the community that lives by faith in the promise of God, and proves that faith by practical and sometimes sacrificial obedience.

The People of God in the Old Testament

If the Church as the biblical people of God began with Abraham, then we need to pay attention to the Old Testament part of its story. We will see how some of the things that Israel believed about themselves in their relationship with God and the world are strongly reflected in what the Christian Church believes about its own existence and mission in the world. Below is a list of some of the key concepts in the Old Testament that governed Israel's sense of identity, and in each case it shows how the New Testament Church inherited the same self-understanding.

Election

The foundation of Israel's faith was that God had chosen them as his own people. They were the seed of Abraham whom God had chosen and called. They were not a nation who had chosen to worship this particular god. Rather, this God had chosen them as his particular people.

They would not exist at all apart from that divine choice and calling.

Two things need to be said immediately. Firstly, the Israelites were not to imagine that their election by God owed anything to their own numerical greatness or moral superiority. Far from it! They were a tiny nation, and no more righteous than other nations. The roots of election lie exclusively in the love and grace of God and for reasons known only to him. (Deuteronomy 7:7-10)

Secondly, they had been chosen, not primarily for their own benefit, but for the sake of the rest of the nations. Blessing Abraham and his descendants was God's intended means of bringing blessing to all nations, which were in a disastrous state. (Genesis 11) Election, then, is not primarily a privilege, but a responsibility. It means being chosen for a task, being a chosen instrument by which God will fulfil his mission of universal blessing.

'You,' said Peter in his letter to the scattered groups of early Christians, 'are a chosen people' (1 Peter 2:9). The Church stands in organic continuity with Israel as the elect people of God. But the same two vital points apply to the New Testament Church as to Old Testament Israel. Such election is entirely by God's grace, not based on anything in us that made us 'choice-worthy'. Election is fundamentally missional in purpose. We are chosen, not so that we alone might enjoy salvation, but so that we can be the means of God's salvation reaching others. The Church exists in the world as the community that God has chosen and called in order to serve God's mission to bring the nations from the situation described in Genesis 4-11 to that portrayed in Revelation 7.

Redemption

Israel knew they were a people whom God had redeemed. They looked back to the great historical deliverance of their ancestors from slavery in Egypt and saw it as the proof of the love, justice, power and incomparable greatness of their God. The language of exodus (redemption, deliverance, mighty acts of justice) filled the worship of Israel, motivated their law and ethics, and inspired hope at both national and personal levels for God's future deliverance. The memory of the exodus was kept alive in the annual Passover celebration. Israel was a people who knew their history. And through their history they knew their God as Redeemer.

The New Testament explicitly sees the cross of Christ through the lens of the exodus (Luke 9:31). On the cross God achieved the redemption of the world, the defeat of the forces of evil, and the liberation of his people. The Christian Church therefore looks back to Calvary as much as Israel did to the exodus. For Christ, our Passover lamb has been sacrificed for us (1 Corinthians 5:7). Christians are people of memory and hope, both of which are focused in their central feast, the Eucharist or Lord's Supper. So the Church stands in organic continuity with Old Testament Israel as the people whom God has redeemed.

Covenant

Another dominant concept in Israel's theology was their covenant relationship with God. This too goes back to Abraham. Covenant involves a promise or commitment on the part of God, and a required response on the part of the one with whom the covenant is made. God promised to bless Abraham, to make him a great nation, and to bless all nations through his descendants. Abraham's response was faith and obedience. God extended this covenant to the whole nation of Israel at Mount Sinai after the exodus. In the same context, God makes known his personal name, Yahweh. This name was forever associated in Israel's mind with the exodus (in which Yahweh proved his redemptive power), and with Sinai (at which Yahweh revealed his character, covenant and law).

Israel understood themselves to be the unique covenant community of Yahweh God. He was committed to them in saving grace, historical protection and blessing, and long-term purpose for the world. They were to be committed to him in sole loyalty and ethical obedience.

Here again there is organic continuity between the testaments. For the Church is the group of people of the new covenant, foretold in the Old Testament and inaugurated by Christ through his death and resurrection. The Church is a community in committed relationship with God. He is committed to those who are united to Christ through faith in his blood, and they are committed to him in exclusive worship and ethical obedience.

Worship

Jesus came to a people who knew how to pray. The people of Israel were committed to worshipping the one living God, and this rich heritage is to be found in the book of Psalms. The language of adoration, praise, thanksgiving, appeal, lament, and protest was well developed in the worshipping life of Israel. So much so, that Moses could ask: what other nation was as close to their god[s] as the lord was close to Israel? (Deuteronomy 4:7)

Naturally, therefore, the Christian Church that sprang from the womb of Old Testament Israel began as a worshipping community. This is one of the most common postures of the Church in the book of Acts – gathered for worship, prayer, and scriptural teaching, just as the Jews did. It is presupposed in all Paul's letters that the churches to which he wrote were fundamentally communities that knew how to worship God, even if their enthusiasm to do so could itself present problems. Worshipping God is the very essence of the Church, and will be so eternally.

Struggle

Old Testament Israel had high ideals, drawn from their covenant relationship with God, but there was nothing idealistic about their historical existence. It is vital to remember that all the truths mentioned above were lived out in the struggle of being an all-too-human society in the midst of the world of nations just as fallen and sinful as Israel itself. So the Old Testament records honestly and painfully Israel's terrible failures alongside all the remarkable affirmations of their faith and aspirations. They sinned and they suffered. They failed internally and they were attacked externally. Their history is a long catalogue of struggle between those who brought the word of God to them and those who were determined to resist the will and ways of their God.

In all of this we see the Church as in a mirror. In the paragraphs that follow we survey many aspects of the Bible's teaching about what the Church is and is meant to be. But we must not lose sight of the fact that whilst the Church is ultimately God's own creation, draws its identity and mission from God, and will accomplish God's purpose; the Church is also a community of sinners – forgiven sinners, yes, but fallen sinners still.

In all these ways, and many more, the Church stands in organic continuity with Old Testament Israel. Of course there are differences; however, the unity of God's people in the Bible is a far more important theological truth than the different periods of their historical existence. Throughout the whole Bible, the people of God are those who are chosen and called by God to serve his purpose of blessing the nations. They are those who have experienced the redeeming grace and power of God in history, ultimately accomplished through Christ on the cross. They are those who stand in committed covenant relationship with God, enjoying the security of his promise and responding in exclusive loyalty and ethical obedience. They are those who are set apart by him and for him to be a distinct and holy community within the surrounding world. They are those who live to worship the living God eternally and yet also live within all the ambiguities of historical life on this sinful planet. In all these things, the Church stands in continuity with Old Testament Israel, because, as Paul puts it, we are sharers in the same promise, the same inheritance and the same good news. (Ephesians 3:6) In Christ Jesus, we belong to the same olive tree. (Romans 11:17-24)

What does the New Testament Say?

The New Testament offers us more than 100 images for the Church. Church traditions have tended to base their ecclesiology on some of them, while neglecting others.

> **Suggested Approach:** Incorporate images of the Church into an integral view so as to establish a framework and common ground for a global understanding of what Church is.

Orlando Costas suggests the use of ***Master Images*** of the Church so as to establish a hermeneutical matrix that includes all images of the Church described in the New Testament.

Such Master Images are: *ecclesia, the people of God, the temple of the Spirit and Body of Christ*[5].

---

5 Reimer 2013:40.

Master Images of the Church

Ecclesia – Gathered to accept responsibility for the world Jesus says that he will build his Church:

> *And I tell you that you are Peter, and on this rock I will build my church, and the gates of Hades will not overcome it.* Matthew 16:18 (NIV)

Jesus calls the Church **ecclesia**. This Greek term used for church means calling out and was used in the ancient world to describe the gathering of citizens of a given city who had the given responsibility to make basic political decisions[6]. Whatever was needed for the city to protect, promote and improve life in the city was discussed and decided on by the ecclesia.

Jesus uses this term as a direct translation of the Hebrew *cahal Jahwe*, which was similarly used in the Old Testament to denote political gatherings for Israel. (1 Chronicles 28:8; 29:1, 10; 2 Chronicles 29:28, 31; 30:2ff, and others[7]). *Cahal* refers to Israel being called to be responsible for the common good of the nation and those who live among them.

> **Ecclesia,** in the view of Jesus, is a ***community of people called out of the world to accept responsibility for the world.***

Jesus calls his disciples *"Salt of the Earth"* and *"Light of the World"*. (Matthew 5:13-15) His followers are called out of the world they no longer belong to (not of this world), but are sent *into* the world to take responsibility for it. (John 17:16-18) They are God's *cahal* with a much greater responsibility for all the nations of the world.

---

6 Coenen 1972:784.
7 Ibid.:785. See Discussion in Reimer 2013:42.

Followers of Christ are to become ambassadors of God, sent to proclaim and demonstrate the Good News of reconciliation with God through Jesus, the Saviour of the world. (2 Corinthians 5:18-20) Whatever they bind and loose on earth will be bound and loosed in heaven. (Matthew 16:19)

It is therefore imperative that wherever the Church of Christ is built, it must orientate and align itself to its ecclesial nature. It is Jesus who builds his Church, establishes it with his own standards. There can be no Church of Christ that does not follow Jesus' description and model.

The *ecclesial* character of the Church presupposes a number of distinctives:

Ecclesia is always a local reality.

We never read about *ecclesia* in a regional or global manner. It is always described in a local context: the church in Jerusalem, the church in Ephesus, or in Rome. As soon as an *ecclesial* reality from a regional perspective is discussed (for example in Asia), a plural form is used – churches. (1 Corinthians 16:19)

Ecclesia covers the whole community

There is no description of a homogenous group of people forming *ecclesia*. It is always a diverse group: men, women, children, poor, rich, Jew and Gentile. (Galatians 3:28). The term refers to a social *territory* and never a social *category* (a selected homogenous group of like-minded, similar social class, culture, ethnicity, language). The diversity of the twelve disciples is a case in point.

Ecclesia describes a responsible gathering facing all issues of communal life

Every issue relevant to the life of the local community is included in the responsibility of *ecclesia*. The mission of *ecclesia* encompasses material, social, cultural and spiritual levels. The Church is life-driven and not task-driven. Her responsibilities include representation and communication of the values of God's Kingdom. The Gospel she preaches and lives out is a Gospel of the Kingdom of God, and it encompasses all of life. (Matthew 4:23; 9:35, Acts:32-35)

The People of God – a Matrix of Life

In the New Testament the Church is described as 'chosen' by God (Ephesians 1:4; Romans 8:33; Colossians 3:12) for a specific purpose. The apostle Peter states:

> *But you are a **chosen people**, a **royal priesthood**, a **holy nation**, a **people belonging** to God, that you may declare the praises of him who called you out of darkness into his wonderful light. Once you were not a people, but now you are the people of God; once you had not received mercy, but now you have received mercy.* 1 Peter 2:8-9 (NIV)

In the Old Testament, Israel was called to be 'a Royal Priesthood' (Exodus 19:6), "God's chosen people (Isaiah 41:8), a people belonging to God (Exodus 3:7, 10:6:7; Leviticus 26:12; 1 Samuel 2:29; 2 Samuel 3:18; 1 Kings 6:13; 2 Kings 20:5; 1 Chronicles 11:2; 2 Chronicles 1:11; Psalms 50:7; Isaiah 1:3; Jeremiah 2:11; Ezekiel 11:20). But Israel disobeyed. Peter refers here to the prophet Hosea who names Israel *Lo-Ammi – Not my people.* (Hosea 1:9), promising a time of grace when they would be again called his holy people. (Hosea 1:10; 2:25). The coming of Jesus marks this time in which God restores a 'people' for himself.

The terms used by Peter to describe this new people are important. Deeply rooted in the Old Testament, they are:

- *Laos* – a holy nation: a nation with a purpose, a nation with a destiny.

- *Genos* – a chosen generation: a people with history, and with a future.

- *Ethnos* – a people with a culture: a socio-cultural space that determines a way of living in a given context.

Together these terms describe a people-group in its totality. This group of people, the people of God, the Church, are a real entity with their own social space and cultural expression, embedded in real communities. Just as Israel was meant to be in the Old Testament, the Church is in the New Testament.

> God's own people: 1 Peter 2:10, Romans 9:25, 2 Corinthians 6:14
>
> God's own nation: 1 Peter 2:9, Titus 2:14
>
> God's own workmanship: Ephesians 2:10
>
> Called to be holy: 1 Corinthians 1:2, Ephesians 4:12
>
> Called to be salt and light: Matthew 5:13
>
> Called for God's glory and to be like him: Ephesians 1:3-13

The Church exists because God wants her to, because God has called her into being. The legitimacy of the Church's existence and her life energy rest in God alone[8]. The Church does not break with God's relations; or walk with humankind as described in the Old Testament, but rather fulfils its promise.

---

8 Moltmann 1967:325; Costas 1974:25; Reimer 2013:56

What does God look like? God looks like, acts like, sounds like and loves like Jesus.

How do we see Jesus today? The Church represents and reflects Jesus on earth.

God made him who had no sin to be sin for us, so that in him we might become the righteousness of God. 2 Cor. 5:21 (NIV)

The Church is called to represent the *"not yet"* in the now: **a new humanity reflecting the new Kingdom of God on earth now.**

How do we reflect Jesus on earth? We do this by being a royal / kingly priesthood.

Two important perspectives are captured here that help us understand the role of the Church:

Royal / Kingly role

Kings are tasked with defining a meaningful structure of life in a given context:

- The shape/appearance of a successful and productive state
- The structure needed to achieve this ideal
- What is considered to be right and wrong behaviour
- How to honour those who do right and punish those who do wrong. (Romans 13:1f)

Kings should be advocates for their people, pursuing a proper social space where a culture of meaningful relationships can evolve and a good life can be enjoyed by all. Without this level of kingly engagement and supportive structures, society would break down.

Priestly role

Priests are concerned with the proper relationship of people to God. Priests become advocates for the establishment of a religious culture that enables a spiritual space through which society can meet and experience God. Their goal is not to invent a production line for righteous individuals, but to enable a new community of people who in their social life embody those qualities of righteousness, peace, justice and love that reflect God's own character and God's original purpose for humanity. Every part of their lives will be affected, and they in turn, they become a blessing in every part of life in society.

The scriptural calling on the Church to be a royal/kingly priesthood indicates three important aspects that help to explain the purpose of the Church:

- **The Church is the voice of righteousness and justice in the world, tasked with bringing and being light to the world.** (This includes bringing light into the institutions, structures and cultures of the world.)

- **The Church is the voice of prayer and intercession for the world,** tasked with standing in the gap on behalf of communities and nations.

- **The Church offers an example of a new humanity, an alternative peoplehood,** living distinct yet fully engaged lives in the community.

This task and calling to be a royal/kingly priesthood, a holy nation, can only be possible under the direct guidance and leadership of God. The Old Testament people called out to take such a role (the Israelites) were governed through a covenantal relationship with God. Similarly, God calls his Church into a covenantal relationship with him, as God's covenant people, sealed and guided by the Holy Spirit (1 Corinthians

3:1f; 2 Corinthians 3:17), through all aspects of life (John 16:14) and through all contexts in time and space.

The position of royal/kingly priesthood comes with significant responsibilities and can be viewed as a powerful role on earth. It is no wonder that religion and state have sought alliances over the years. However, the church is called to be in the world, not of the world; she is called to be different. In Hebrews 13:14 we understand that our city is not of the world. So, though the Church is everywhere on earth, her permanent home is in heaven. The Church submits only to God. The Church identifies and accepts responsibility for all people, loves all people, seeks the best (life in all its fullness/*shalom*) for all people, disciples all people to follow Christ (Matthew 28:19-20), yet never identifies with any people. The Church in her role to be God's alternative people must demonstrate the new humanity in God's Kingdom, a role that requires serving, not ruling. The Church of God is in all regards an eschatological people, as her rule is with Christ in heaven. (Revelation 20:4-5)

A Temple of the Spirit – A Place to meet God

The Church is God's House (1 Peter 4:17; 1 Timothy 3:15). God dwells in her. He promised Israel to live and walk among his chosen people (Leviticus 26:11-12). And when Israel left him and was dispersed to many nations of the world, God promised to return to Zion, gather Israel there and dwell again among his people (Zechariah 2:10-15; Zephaniah 3:15-17; Psalm 68:17-18). Nations would come and join Israel in Zion and see God's Glory among his people (Isaiah 68:16; Jeremiah 3:17). The basic truth – that God dwells among his people – is fulfilled in the Church in full consistency with the Old Testament.

The Church is God's dwelling place. This image is often used in the New Testament and points to six basic truths about the Church:

Truth	Impact
The Church belongs to God (1 Corinthians 3:9). No one else may claim ownership. God alone is her owner. All authority over the Church belongs to God.	• This excludes all national and denominational ambitions. • There can be no national Church. • No church planter, no bishop or patriarch, not even a pope, no synod and no board may claim to be the last authority in ecclesial matters.
God lives in the Church (Ephesians 2:19). She is the place of his dwelling. (Note: this does not refer to a building, but to a people)	• As God lives in the Church, the Church is holy (1 Corinthians 3:16). • Wherever God lives there is truth (1 Timothy 3:14-15) and righteousness (2 Corinthians 5:21). • Living together with God and one another, people grow into the fullness of love and become more godlike (Ephesians 3:14ff).
The triune God builds the Church (Acts 20:32) in Jesus (Matthew 16:18) as ecclesia, a fellowship of people called out from the world to accept responsibility for the world, and in the form of the temple of the Spirit. (1 Corinthians 3:16)	• Mission of the Father: a heart of love for the world sends the beloved Son to the world. • Mission of Christ: brings salvation and redemption, calls out his ecclesia and sends them into the world. • Mission of the Spirit: empowers, trains, transforms, distinctive. 2 Corinthians 3:17
The Church God builds is an apostolic and prophetic reality. She is built on an apostolic and prophetic foundation (Ephesians 2:20).	• God builds a missional Church sent to proclaim and demonstrate the Gospel of the Kingdom to the world with prophetic clarity.

God builds his Church through humans. The stone on which he builds are people like Peter (Matthew 16:18). Jesus himself is the cornerstone; they all build the rest of the structure.

- We are living building blocks forming his wonderful structure.
- Each in his or her place, for each one is God's workmanship created for the good works he has prepared for them to do (Ephesians 2:10).
- They are gifted by the Spirit to work for the common good (1 Corinthians 12:7).
- Wherever the gifts of the Spirit are used in ministry, the church is built (1 Corinthians 14:12).

God will finish building his Church. As the bride of Christ, completion will occur when Jesus comes to take his bride home.

- At present the Church is being built, never done, always in process. Orlando Costas calls the church a *'reality and a missionary project.'*
- It is being perfectly built and still in the process of being finished.
- As everyone may imagine, a building site is never clean, never sterile, and always messy.

The house of God is a place where people from all the corners of the world may meet with God. They should recognise him in the ***living stones*** that form the body of Christ. They see him in and through the *good works of the church members.* (Matthew 5:16) They encounter God through the ministry of the priests in the temple, who serve God interceding for the world around them. (1 Peter 2:5)

Body of Christ – The Fullness of Competence

God reveals himself in history. To see and understand the heart of God we need to explore the story of God's people. The whole Bible is full of stories of God's people: how he calls, engages with, relates to them and, in turn, how they respond to God. He is the God of Abraham, Isaac and Jacob (Exodus 6:3). He is with Moses and the people during their Exodus from Egypt (Exodus 33:12-17) and throughout the history of his people. This climaxes in God revealing himself in Jesus Christ (Hebrews 1:1) to reconcile the world with himself (2 Corinthians 5:18-20) and display to humans God's glory (John 1: 14).

The Church is the *'Body of Christ'* (1 Corinthians 12:27; Ephesians 1:23). She is built by Christ (Matthew 16:18) and sent by Christ as the Father sent him (John 20:21). The Father sent him, the eternal word of God, God himself as an incarnated human (John 1:1). Jesus became a human being in order that we may see the glory of God (John 1:14). Similarly, the Church is an incarnated reality in the midst of human cultures. She is by her very nature *humanic* and as such, contextual. Her formal structures should therefore adapt to the context in which she is built. Apostle Paul speaks of Jewish expressions for the Jews, Greek for the Greek and even Barbarian for the Barbarians (1 Corinthians 9:19-22). In her very nature, God displays his nature; just as he promised to do with Israel in the Old Testament.

She is, culturally speaking, highly flexible, because of her somatic nature. It is less the form, the offices, that identify her members, but the Spirit who grants them gifts, which determine their ministries and their place in this organic structure (1 Corinthians 12:4-6,13). Led by Christ, the head (Colossians 1:18; Ephesians 1:22f; Romans 12:5), this organic network represents the most powerful organisation on Earth because it has within her the fullness of all lives. (Ephesians 1:23)

Other Images of the Church in the New Testament

There are a number of other images in the New Testament. All of them follow the pattern established above. All of them derive their symbolic value and theological content from the Old Testament.

The Church is, for example, called a **flock of sheep** of which Jesus is the shepherd (John 10:1-10). No one joins them except through Jesus, the door, who gave his life for the sheep (John 10:11-15). She is a **planting of God** (1 Cor. 3:9), and **vineyard** planted by God (Matthew 21:33-43) where God is the owner (John 15:1-5). The Church is a **blameless bride** of the Lamb of God (Revelations 19:7), loved by Christ who offered his life for her. (Ephesians 5:26)

Many other images can be added. They all depict a spiritual, organic network built and owned by God to fulfil God's will on earth.

The People of God in the New Testament[9]

Tracing the story of God's people from the Old Testament to the New Testament demonstrates God's ongoing intention to have a people called out to be his witness. The person of Jesus Christ becomes the central and defining presence, to which all his followers relate. Jesus comes as the fulfilment of the promise of God in the Old Testament, so the followers of Jesus are those who live in the light of that fulfilment.

---

9 Reflections from Dr Christopher Wright linking the Old and New Testament

The time is fulfilled

In the earliest recorded preaching of Jesus (Mark 1:15), we hear the note of fulfilment that dominates the Gospels. Throughout the Old Testament period and beyond, the people of Israel grew in expectation that their God would bring about a new state of affairs in human history, and they looked forward to that future with hope.

That hope is now fulfilled, said the New Testament writers, through what was inaugurated in the life, death and resurrection of Jesus. As Messiah, God's anointed one, Jesus embodied Israel in his own person – taking on their destiny and fulfilling their mission. In his life and teaching he inaugurated the kingdom of God, demonstrating the power of God's reign in word and deed. In his death he took upon himself the judgment of God against sin, not just on behalf of his own people Israel, but for the whole world. In his resurrection, God fulfilled his promise to redeem Israel. As Paul put it, *'what God promised our fathers he has fulfilled for us, their children, by raising up Jesus.'* (Acts 13:32) Before his ascension, Jesus commissioned his followers to carry forward the Abrahamic mission of Israel, now focused on the name of Christ himself, to bring the blessings of repentance and forgiveness to all nations. (Luke 24:46-47). To empower them for this, the risen Christ sent the Holy Spirit, whose outpouring had been prophesied as a sign of God's new age of salvation and blessing. (Isaiah 32:15-20; Joel 2:28-32).

The outpouring of the Spirit of God at Pentecost demonstrated that the new era of fulfilment had begun. The crucifixion, resurrection and ascension of Jesus of Nazareth had accomplished what God promised. Those who responded in repentance and faith could now belong to the restored Israel in Christ, whether they were Jews like his first followers, or Gentiles from the nations who were now also invited to belong to this new community.

As the community of those who have responded to God's action in Jesus Christ, the Church is described in the New Testament by several simple terms. These terms were used even before the term 'Christian' was invented, and they remain perennially true as descriptions of all members of the Church, as they are all related to Jesus.

Disciples

The original nucleus of the Christian church in the New Testament was the group of disciples of Jesus. 'Disciples' means learners – those who are the followers and adherents of a teacher or master. From the Gospels we learn that there were three main aspects to being disciples of Jesus, all of which are still marks of belonging to his Church.

- First, disciples are those whom Jesus has called to himself, to be with him. This is not just following the teaching of a dead leader. To be a disciple is to be in a constant relationship with Jesus; or rather, it is to experience the truth of the last promise he made to his disciples, 'I am with you always.' (Matthew 28:20)

- Second, disciples are those who obey Jesus. It is a matter of personal loyalty, in which we take all Jesus said with great seriousness, and submit to his authority. That means submission of mind, heart and will to Jesus Christ.

- Third, disciples are commissioned and sent out by Jesus, in his name (which means, with his authority), to make disciples of the nations. That is, discipleship is a self-replicating mission.

Jesus had a special group of twelve disciples, eleven of whom later became known as apostles. But the Gospels also speak of a wider group of disciples, ordinary followers of Jesus. Though the word 'disciple' itself is not greatly used in the New Testament after the Gospels, it is clear that the Church is always a community of disciples, the followers of

Jesus who live with his presence, submit to his teaching, and carry forward his mission.

Witnesses

'*You are my witnesses,*' said Jesus to his disciples, after his resurrection and before his ascension (Luke 24:48; Acts 1:8). Jesus was almost certainly echoing the words that God had spoken to Israel in Isaiah (43:10-12). Israel was supposed to be the people who bore witness among the surrounding nations to the reality of their God, Yahweh. The nations would come to know who God really is from the testimony of those to whom he entrusted the task of witnessing.

Similarly, Jesus entrusts the truth about himself to those who had witnessed him. Originally, of course, the words were spoken to the first apostles, who had personally witnessed the life, teaching, death and resurrection of Jesus. (Acts 3:15) But by extension, all Christians are called to bear witness to what they have experienced of the saving love of God in Christ. The Church is the guardian of that apostolic witness. Sometimes the cost of bearing that witness is high, as the earliest Christians found, and countless others down the centuries have proved. The word *martyr* originally meant simply, 'witness'. But since that witness so often ended in death at the hands of those who rejected it, the meaning changed to '*one who gives his or her life rather than compromise their testimony.*'

Believers

The next common description of the earliest Christians (before they got that name) as 'believers' is in the book of Acts. This term too goes back to the Gospels, because Jesus so frequently called for faith, along with repentance. Faith is the key to entering the kingdom of God, and to receiving its blessings, including forgiveness, healing, and eternal life. Faith too, like discipleship and witness, is entirely directed to the person of Jesus himself. It is not just a matter of believing certain propositions, though it does include believing the claims of Christ. Rather, it means an act of personal trust in God, focused on Jesus as the one who has fulfilled God's promises and who died and rose again for our salvation. The Church, then, is essentially a community of disciples of Christ, witnesses to Christ, and believers in Christ.

Pictures of the Church

The Church is much more than just a collection of individuals who claim to be disciples of, witnesses to, and believers in Jesus Christ. The church as a whole is a significant entity. It is a historical reality in the world, with its spiritual roots going right back to Abraham. The Bible provides many metaphors to convey different aspects of this reality. Most of them are found in the Old Testament as ways of describing Israel, and are then extended in the New Testament to those who are in Christ. One metaphor, however, the concept of the Church as a body, or as the body of Christ, is unique to the New Testament.

A household or family

Old Testament Israel was a kinship-structured society, divided into tribes, clans and households. The basic unit in this arrangement was the 'father's house' or *beth-ab*. This was the extended family, of three or even four generations, including married sons and their children, household servants, agricultural workers and even resident foreigners practising their trade. This robust organism provided the individual Israelite with vital support. The household was the place in which the individual found personal identity and inclusion (personal names always included the father's house, as well as clan and tribal names). It was the place of security, since the household had its inherited portion of the land. And it was the place of spiritual nurture and teaching in the law of God. Already in Old Testament times, the whole nation of Israel could be metaphorically described as a household: 'House of Israel' or 'House of Yahweh', picturing the whole group as an extended family belonging to God.

It is not surprising that the early Christians adopted similar language to speak of the Church community. Paul calls it 'the household of God'. (1 Timothy 3:15) 'We are his house', says the writer to the Hebrews (3:6). Applying this metaphor was undoubtedly made even easier by the fact that the first Christians met in homes, and the sense of being an extended family must have been strong. As in the Old Testament, the Church as a household was the place of identity (in Christ), inclusion (in the fellowship of sisters and brothers), security (in an eternal inheritance), and nurture and teaching (in the scriptures and teaching of the apostles). For those who had been severed from their natural family connections because of loyalty to Christ, the Church as a new family in all these senses was, and still is, of great importance.

A people

Old Testament Israel most often referred to themselves as a people (*'am*) defined more by community than by ethnicity. In fact, although the core of Israel was the ethnically-related community descended from the twelve tribes of the sons of Jacob/Israel, it was a very mixed society (cf. Exodus 12:37; Joshua 9; Leviticus 19:33-34). What held Israel together was not so much single ethnicity as covenant loyalty to the one God, Yahweh. So they were above all 'the people of Yahweh'. But that title could be expanded. The Old Testament envisaged people of other nations coming to be included in the people of Yahweh (Isaiah 19:24-25; Psalms 87; Zechariah 2:11) – and that is exactly what the New Testament says has happened through the mission of the Church.

So the Church is a people, or rather it is *the* people of the biblical God, through faith in Christ. But it is also a multi-national people, in which membership is open to all, Jew and Gentile, male and female, slave and free (Galatians 3:28). So the language that had first applied to Israel is now extended to people of all nations. 'You,' says Peter, 'are a people belonging to God...once you were not a people, but now you are the people of God.' (1 Peter 2:9-10) As a worldwide community of people, the Church fulfils the promise of God to Abraham and anticipates the ultimate gathering of God's people in the new creation (Revelation 7:9, 21:3).

A bride

The relationship between Yahweh and his people, being one of love, is portrayed in terms of the marriage covenant. Hosea seems to have been the first to make that comparison. The metaphor could also be used negatively to accuse Israel of being an unfaithful bride (Hos. 2; Jer. 2:1-2; Ezek. 16). Nevertheless, it is clear that God wants a people who are bonded to him in mutual loving devotion, as husband and wife ideally should be.

In the New Testament the Church is portrayed as the Bride of Christ. On the one hand, the metaphor highlights Christ's love for the Church, and especially his self-giving, sacrificial care for his Bride. On the other hand, it speaks of the beauty and adornment of the Bride, who will one day be perfect and without blemish for her divine husband (Ephesians 5:25-27; Revelation 21:2). In both directions, the picture is one of love, commitment, beauty and celebration. (Revelation 19:9).

A priesthood

'You will be for me a priestly kingdom,' said God to Israel at Mount Sinai. (Exodus 19:6) Priests stood between God and the rest of the people.

They operated as mediator in both directions. On the one hand they taught the law of God to the people. On the other hand they brought the people's sacrifices to God. Through the priests, God came to the people. Through the priests, the people came to God. And it was also the job of the priests to bless the people in the name of Yahweh. (Numbers 6:22-27) Then, by analogy, God tells Israel that they will stand in a similar position between him and the rest of the nations of the earth. Through Israel, God will become known to the nations (Isaiah 42:1-7; 49:1-6). And through Israel, God will ultimately draw the nations to himself (Isaiah 2:1-5; 60:1-3; Jeremiah 3:17). Israel's priesthood among the nations would fulfil the Abrahamic role of blessing them.

The priestly identity of Old Testament Israel is now inherited by those who are in Christ (1 Peter 2:9-12). As God's priesthood, the Church consists of those who are to declare the praises of God and what he has done. And as a holy priesthood, Christians are to live in such a way that the nations are drawn to praise God for themselves. Priesthood is a missional concept, for it puts the Church between God and the world with the task of bringing the two together in Christ – making God known to the nations, and calling the nations to repentance and faith in God and to the sacrifice of the cross. This double direction of movement seems to have been in Paul's mind when he spoke of his own missionary work as a 'priestly duty' in Romans 15:16.

A temple

The temple in Jerusalem was one of the central pillars of Israel's faith and identity. It had a dual significance.

Firstly, the temple, like the tabernacle before it, was regarded as the place of God's dwelling. Israel knew, of course, that the creator of the universe did not actually live in any little house they had built, nor did he need to (1 Kings 8:27; 2 Samuel 7:1-7). Nevertheless, this temple was the place that God had chosen to make his dwelling (1 Kings 8:29), and where his glory would be tangibly felt.

"I will keep my covenant with you ... I will put my dwelling-place among you, and I will not abhor you. I will walk among you and be your God, and you will be my people." (Leviticus 26:9-12).

Secondly, the temple was a place where Israelites would come to meet with God, as the tabernacle had been called a 'tent of meeting'. God was everywhere, but the temple provided a 'direction' for their prayer (1 Kings 8), and pilgrimage to the temple in Jerusalem became significant and joyful, though never obligatory. Psalms 120-134 are songs for such pilgrimage, and they express the joy (in the midst of struggles too), of knowing, meeting, trusting, and worshipping God in Zion – the place where the temple stood and where God's people celebrated his presence – provided they did so with moral integrity. (Psalms 15, 24; Isaiah 1:10-17; Jeremiah 7:1-15)

Jesus, as the Lord's anointed messiah and king, had fulfilled God's purpose for Israel, and this had major implications for the physical temple. Jesus himself took over its double role. Jesus is the person (no longer the place) in whom God's presence is among us as Immanuel, and through whom people must now come to meet God in worship (John 4:2-26). The writer to the Hebrews points out that by coming to Christ, Christians have already come to Mount Zion (to the temple), just as in him they have an altar, the perfect sacrifice, and God's great High Priest (Hebrews 12:22).

Paul goes further and sees the Church itself as the temple of God. Not in the sense of a physical building (Christians did not start building 'churches' for a long time after the New Testament period), but rather, the Church as the community in which God dwells by his Spirit, and where people gather to meet with God – the double function of the

Old Testament temple.

Paul uses the temple imagery at three distinct levels: the individual Christian, the local church, and the whole Church, but all with the basic idea of a dwelling place for God.

- In **1 Corinthians 6:19** Paul warns Christians that they cannot use their bodies in any way they like, especially not for sexual immorality, for *'your body is a temple of the Holy Spirit.'* This is the only individual application of the concept.

- In **1 Corinthians 3:16-17** Paul extends the picture to include the local Christians in Corinth as, collectively, God's temple. Similarly, in 2 Corinthians 6:16 Paul warns the Corinthians that they must not take part in things that were connected with pagan temples, *'for we are the temple of the living God.'*

- In **Ephesians 2:21-22** Paul addresses Gentile believers, explaining how they have now been united with believing Jews into one single community through the death of Christ. He uses temple imagery to describe how all Christians, Jews and Gentiles, are being built together into a temple for God to dwell in by his Spirit.

The temple image as applied to the Church implies that there is only one Church: the people of the one living God, who has only one dwelling place, through his one Spirit. There was only one temple in Old Testament Israel. But God promised that it would be 'a house of prayer for all nations' (Isaiah 56:7) and Solomon prayed for it to be a place of blessing for foreigners when it was first dedicated (1 Kings 8:41-43). Now, through Christ and the gospel, that was a reality. The temple of God is now truly the multi-national community of believers from all nations.

A vine and an olive tree

Two pictures of the people of God are drawn from horticulture. Both in the Old and New Testaments, they are compared to a vine and an olive tree. Jesus uses the first and Paul the second.

In John 15, Jesus says he is the true vine. He is referring to the fact that in the Old Testament, Israel is likened to a vine that the Lord God had planted in his own land (Psalm 80). Unfortunately, God's expectations from his vine were smashed. Isaiah pictures God looking for a harvest of good grapes from his people to reward his loving investment in them, but instead of justice, finds bloodshed, and instead of righteousness, cries of the oppressed (Isaiah 5:1-7; cf. Ezekiel 15).

Jesus is similarly concerned about the fruitfulness of his followers. Abiding in Christ is the only way to being fruitful.

In Romans 11:13-36 Paul compares Israel to an olive tree (Jeremiah 11:16; Hosea 14:6). Paul, however, builds a whole theology around the horticultural practice of stripping some branches off a tree and grafting in others, in order to rejuvenate the original tree and increase its fruit-bearing. Paul sees an analogy to the way Gentiles are being grafted into the original covenant people of God, Israel, while some of those original people were being cut off because they failed to respond to what God had now done in Jesus Christ.

It is important to note that God's response to the failure of many Jews to believe in Jesus was not to chop down the olive tree and plant a completely new one. Some branches may be lopped off, and other branches wonderfully grafted in, but the roots and the trunk remain. Paul thus confirms the continuity between Old Testament Israel and the Church, and the unity of believing Jews and Gentiles in the one new people of God. There is only one olive tree, only one covenant people of God throughout both testaments and all of history. There also remains the opportunity for branches that have been cut off to be grafted in again, if they turn in repentance and faith to God through Christ.

A flock

Another picture of the Church that is found in both testaments is also drawn from the world of agriculture – a flock of sheep. It is, perhaps, not a very flattering image, but it is used in two significant ways, depending on who is pictured as the shepherd or shepherds.

God as Shepherd: 'We are his people, the sheep of his pasture.' (Psalms 100:3). The main point of this metaphor was to highlight God's providential and tender care for his people, as a shepherd cares for his flock. Individuals could take comfort from this (Psalm 23), but the whole nation could envisage itself being led by their divine Shepherd (Isaiah 40:11).

Leaders as shepherds: It was common to speak of kings as shepherds of their people. Care, provision, guidance and protection were expected of them – in theory at least. In reality, in Israel, the complaint was that their 'shepherds' more often exploited the sheep than cared for them. Ezekiel vigorously condemns such shepherds (meaning the kings of Israel), and says that God himself will take on the job of shepherding his own flock again (Ezekiel 34).

It is against this background that Jesus claimed to be the good, or model, shepherd in John 10:31-33. This was not just a promise of tender care as in Psalms 23. It was a bold claim to be the true king of Israel, to be the divine king himself, as promised by Ezekiel. Not surprisingly, it led to a violent reaction (John 10:31-33). But Jesus went on to describe his followers (i.e. the embryonic church) as his own known sheep, and then pointed forward to the inclusion of others, within a single flock under a single shepherd (John 10:16 – echoing Ezekiel 37:22-24).

As a natural extension, those who are called to leadership within the Church are portrayed as shepherds also. Peter calls them 'under-shepherds' of the Chief Shepherd, who is Jesus. Christian leaders are to work with love, without greed, with servant hearts, and as good examples to the rest of the flock (1 Peter 5:1-4). Paul adds the additional duty of defending the flock from ravaging wolves – his matching metaphor for false teachers who seek to devour the sheep (Acts 20:28).

A body

Finally, we come to the one major picture of the Church that is unique to the New Testament and unique to Paul – that is, the Church as a body, or specifically as the 'body of Christ'.

We note four key points that emerge from Paul's rich development of this picture of the Church:

- **Unity and diversity of members:** Paul first uses the human body simply as a very effective simile. In 1 Corinthians 12:12-30, he likens the believers within the Church to the different parts of the human body. There are many physical parts of a body, but they all cohere within the one body; they all assist one another; they all experience joy or pain together; and they all contribute to the healthy functioning of the body as a single organism. His main point in this context is that God has arranged things in this way for the good of the whole. No single part should think that it is so important that it has no need of any other part of the body; and no single part should consider itself less important than some other more prominent part. Paul's point in relation to the Church is that all the spiritual gifts God has distributed among different members of the Church are given for the benefit of the whole. So, in Romans 12:4-8, using the same comparison, he urges those with different gifts to use them wholeheartedly and with humility. There is diversity within the Church, but it exists within the fundamental unity that we all belong to the one Christ and share the one Spirit. The Church, like the human body, is an organic unit with functional diversity.

- **Christ as the head:** The main emphasis in 1 Corinthians 12 and Romans 12 is on the horizontal relationships within the body. But in Colossians and Ephesians, Paul develops the picture in a more vertical direction by speaking of Christ as the head, in such a way that the Church relates to Christ, just as the rest of the human body is related to the head. There seem to be three elements to this picture.

First, in both letters Paul puts this description of Christ as the head of his body, the Church, in the same context as Christ's sovereignty over the whole of creation (Colossians 1:15-18; Ephesians 1:19-22). The implication is that Christ exercises Lordship and control over the Church. This, however, as Paul stresses elsewhere, is a headship that is exercised in tender love and servanthood, with self-sacrificial, self-giving care (Ephesians 5:23-30).

Second, in Ephesians 1:23 Paul speaks of Christ 'filling the Church' as his body, just as he fills the whole of creation. For example, our minds are aware of our bodies, as present in each action and function, in each cell, muscle and tissue. Likewise, Christ is present everywhere and active within his Church.

Third, just as a body grows as a living organism under the direction of the head, so Paul describes the Church as growing up, both from and into Christ (Colossians 2:19; Ephesians 4:12-14). The body metaphor is useful for Paul's passion for maturity among his churches. As a body cannot grow if it is severed from its head, neither can the Church grow if it does not remain vitally connected to Christ.

- **Reconciliation of Jew and Gentile:** The most fundamental division at the time was between Jews and Gentiles. And it was central to Paul's understanding of the Gospel and of the Church that God had removed that barrier through the death of Jesus the Messiah. So in Ephesians 2:14-18 he describes how God has brought both together by uniting the two in a single new humanity through the cross and by presenting them both together to God. He uses, body language, again, saying that Christ's intention was 'in this one body to reconcile both of them to God through the cross, by which he put to death their hostility' (v 16). This 'one body' clearly means the Church of believing and reconciled Jews and Gentiles in Christ. This was so important to Paul that he seems to have coined a new Greek word to describe it in Ephesians 3:6, where he says that Gentiles constitute a 'co-body' (*syssoma*) with Israel, as well as being co-heirs and co-sharers in the promise in Christ Jesus. The Church in this sense is a new and unprecedented reality in history: nothing less than a new humanity - a new body.

- **Appropriate behaviour.** There is no place among the members of the same body for either a superiority complex (rejecting others as less important than oneself), or an inferiority complex (rejecting oneself as of no importance in comparison with others). This is the message of 1 Corinthians 12: 14-26. Paul takes the metaphor in an even more positive direction to speak about Christian behaviour within the Church. In Ephesians 4:15-16, 23, Christians should speak the truth in love with one another, because they are to be growing up in love as a whole body under Christ, and 'we are all members of one body'.

We have explored the major biblical pictures or metaphors of the Church as the people of God. We should not set one up as dominant, at the expense of the others, or neglect any of them. Also, we should

Missionary by Nature

WHAT is the purpose of the Church here on earth? The images examined so far in the New Testament clearly point to the following facts:

> The Church is God's people, called out of the world to be responsible for the world.
>
> The Church is God's missionary agent sent to all corners of the world to represent, demonstrate and preach the Gospel of the Kingdom.
>
> The Church is an organic structure and network of people gifted by the Spirit of God to serve God and the world for his glory and the growth of his Kingdom.

Everything the church is and does is aiming to fulfil God's own mission on earth. She is missionary by her very nature. In today's world we call her missional[10]. The difference between missionary and missional churches is clear: 'the missionary churches do mission (among other activities), the missional – are mission'[11]. McNeal states it clearly when he says: "The missional church is not what but who?"[12] She defines the reason of being through the mission of God to the world[13]. And this means the missional Church is characterised by her relationship:

- To God (*coram Deo*).

---

10   Barrett 2006:178f; Reimer 2013a:70-71.
11   Reimer 2013a:71.
12   McNeal 2009:20.
13   Frost 2003:225.

not imagine that these are pictures only of some idealised or mystical church. These are ways in which the Old Testament speaks about historical Israel, and the New Testament speaks about the actual assemblies of Christian believers in the early Church. Both Israel and the Church were filled with very ordinary people with many faults and failures. By means of these metaphors and images, however, God reminded them of the real identity that they had, and emphasised different aspects of their relationship with Christ and with each other. We need all of these teachings and models to inform our understanding of what we mean by the 'whole Church.'

All this supports the basic idea of the **Church's missionary nature.**

- To the world (*coram mundo*)¹⁴.

She is only God's Church when her relationship to God and the world is rightly established, and she lives under the leadership of God the Spirit (2 Corinthians 3:17) in the midst of the world, doing what God intends to do in and with the world.

This missionary nature of the Church establishes the major characteristics of the Church; she is spiritual, contextual and integral.

Christ Incarnate

The Church is the 'Body of Christ' (Ephesians 1:23), created by the Spirit, who implants or grafts in the individual members of the body through an act of a spiritual baptism (1 Corinthians 12:13). As such, the Church is not of this world (John 15:19). She is Spirit-made, Spirit-guided, a spiritual reality. It would be completely wrong to identify the Church as just one more societal institution. In God's view she needs to be preserved as holy, without blame (Ephesians 5:27) and clearly distanced from organisational patterns that the world follows (Romans 12:2). She is a place where God, her creator, lives and there is no greater importance for her than living for the glory of God (Ephesians 1:3ff). The missional church represents God in her midst. And whatever she is and does, she is and does in him.

The missional church never does her own thing; never works to satisfy her own interests and programmes. She is with God and follows him in everything. And it is God who cares for her needs, God who satisfies her basic desires. God is her Father.

In Luke 11:11-13 we read: *"Which of you fathers, if your son asks for a fish, will give him a snake instead? Or if he asks for an egg, will give him a scorpion? If you then, though you are evil, know how to give good gifts*

14   McNeal 2009:183.

to your children, how much more will your Father in heaven give the Holy Spirit to those who ask him?"

God cares for his Church because only through his care will she be able to accomplish her task on earth. Without God she can do nothing (John 15:5). God is the conduit for her effectiveness and spiritual success.

The Church Incarnate

The Church is a spiritual reality, but also an incarnate reality in this world. Jesus underlines the fact by saying:

"They are not of the world, just as I am not of the world. Sanctify them by your truth. Your word is truth. As you sent me into the world, I also have sent them into the world. And for their sakes I sanctify myself, that they also may be sanctified by the truth." (John 17:16-19)

The Church is not of the world, but she is sent into the world. The world is the place where she engages. And she does this in human terms. She is human by nature. Her members are humans among humans, her means are means of human culture and her forms are socio-cultural forms. She is among people. And the world she is in is first and foremost the local community. The Church is *ecclesia*, a local assembly of believers called out to accept responsibility for the place in which she is living.

For the Jews in Jerusalem there must be a Jewish Jerusalem Church, for the Greeks in Ephesus a Greek Ephesus Church. A missional Church is this local *ecclesia*. This means there can never be a global unified Church structure and form. The Church of Christ is in principle contextual. She adapts the language and cultural form, is understood by the local people, and becomes flesh amongst the people in order that the local community may see the glory of God among them and understand. A missional understanding of the Church creates the opportunity to plant churches all around the world, preaching and demonstrating the only true gospel in varieties of ways, languages and forms.

The New Testament is the best witness for the splendid diversity of ecclesial expressions. Compare the first church congregations in Jerusalem and Antioch and take, for example, their leadership forms. The church in Jerusalem was led by apostles and deacons (Acts 6:1ff), while in Antioch prophets and teachers exercised leadership (Acts 13:1ff). Both are churches established by the work of the Holy Spirit, in both apostles of Christ were active, but the applied leadership was clearly different, because the context in which the gospel was preached differed radically. Context impacts structure.

There is no unified ecclesiological format in the New Testament because there is no unified culture in the world. And the Church, being a body of Christ, follows Jesus in incarnating into a culture, becoming as human as possible to display the glory of God to people in their own language and culture. This is the way Christ is presented to them.

The local nature of the Church always includes the total local *ethnos*. To divide the social space into homogeneous groups, as suggested by the church growth movement, for the sake of evangelism is biblically irresponsible. Nowhere in the New Testament is such an approach taught. The concept is theologically and missiologically problematic, as David Shenk points out in his study on the consequences of the theory for the Muslim world. The concentration on certain groups in society will soon create what C. Wayne Zunkel once called 'People and Kingdom blindness'. The Church will lose sight of the people around her, unable to see the context she is in, and by missing the target she will be unable to develop a Kingdom presence in that context.

All for All

People are at the head of God's mission in the world. God's mission is motivated by selfless love (John 3:16) seeking restoration of humans into his image. To achieve this, God sent Jesus Christ into the world, and through Jesus, reconciled himself with the world (2 Corinthians 5:18). Following Jesus, the Church concentrates on reconciliation of the world with God. The whole world! Her mission can never concentrate on parts of humanity, nor even only on humanity. She is a messenger of reconciliation to the world. To the Corinthians the apostle Paul writes:

"All this is from God, who reconciled us to himself through Christ and gave us the ministry of reconciliation: that God was reconciling the world to himself in Christ, not counting people's sins against them. And he has committed to us the message of reconciliation. We are therefore Christ's ambassadors, as though God were making his appeal through us. We implore you on Christ's behalf: Be reconciled to God. God made him who had no sin to be sin for us, so that in him we might become the righteousness of God." (2 Corinthians 5:18-21)

The Church is an ambassador of reconciliation sent to the world with a word of hope to all creation. Nobody is excluded. 'All creation waits for the revelation of the children of God' (Romans 8:19). It is crucial to see that the whole world is the subject of God's mission and, consequently, also of the mission of the Church. This is so important and means that all church members are to be involved in God's mission. No one is excluded; they are all made as God's best workmanship to do the works He has made for them to do. (Ephesians 2:10) The body of Christ will grow as soon as the individual members of the Church start to support each other in fulfilling God's mission in the world. (Ephesians 4:16)

Mission is a collective venture of the whole Church to the whole world.

In the Church of Christ no one is left out, nobody is more important than the other, no one is only a receiver or only a giver, no one can lean back and rest and observe while others work for the wellbeing of the world. Everybody is gifted by the Spirit of God, called into ministries of the Lord and empowered to do works of God in the world for the common good of all. (1 Corinthians 12:4-7)

This is especially significant as we look at the division in the world today between the wealthy and the economically poor. The imbalance is striking. But does this worldly power translate to more spiritual authority? Gifts of the Spirit do not require money or education. The only thing needed is the total dedication of one's life to God. Even the poorest and the illiterate can receive the gift of an apostle, prophet, evangelist, teacher and healer. The Spirit distributes his gifts according to his will. No more – no less. And this means that even the poor and the less privileged of the world can be spiritually strong and more than able to contribute to the mission of God to the world. As a matter of fact, God generally uses those less economically privileged to do his marvellous works of grace in the world. Amazed at this discovery, the apostle Paul writes to the Corinthians who tended to compete for the most powerful and best leader:

"Brothers and sisters, think of what you were when you were called. Not many of you were wise by human standards; not many were influential; not many were of noble birth. But God chose the foolish things of the world to shame the wise; God chose the weak things of the world to shame the strong. God chose the lowly things of this world and the despised things—and the things that are not—to nullify the things that are, so that no one may boast before him. It is because of him that you are in Christ Jesus, who has become for us wisdom from God—that is, our righteousness, holiness and redemption. Therefore, as it is written: "Let the one who boasts boast in the Lord." (1 Corinthians 1:26-31)

God does not need the wisdom and the riches of the world. Those who boast of such things will go away empty. Jesus needs no more than five loaves of bread and two fishes to feed a crowd of 5,000 men and possibly as many women and children. For God, enough was simply what a small boy carried in his bag (Mark 6:1ff).

The global Church has to learn this lesson. She is God's Church. And God decides what to give whom. We will do well to accept our gift and use it faithfully. No more is expected of a faithful servant. (1 Corinthians. 4:1)

Mission with the People

The whole Church is sent to the whole world. Her mission is in the world. She is there for the world. It is widely accepted in missiological circles that mission requires involvement, contextualisation and inculturation. You cannot reach people with the Gospel without learning their language, rituals, values and other religious and cultural settings. Only when we understand the people will we start to communicate meaningfully. The mission of the Church is for the people and the Church is 'a community for the world',[15] or as Dietrich Bonhoeffer puts it, "*The Church is the Church only when it exists for others ... The Church must share in the secular problems of ordinary human life, not dominating, but helping and serving.*" [16]

But how do we find inroads into a foreign culture? How do we become a Church for others, without falling into the syndrome of 'pro-existence' as Theo Sundermeier, reflecting on Bonhoeffer's phrase and its liberal-humanist background, critically observes?[17] Too often the 'Church for others' thought they knew better what others needed, and

---

15 Barth 1962:762ff.
16 Bonhoeffer 1971:382f. Translation in Bosch 2011:384.
17 Sundermeier 1986:62ff. See also Bosch 2011:384.

the helper soon dominated those in need of help. Sundermeier suggested, instead of talking about a Church for others, we should speak of 'the Church with others'.[18] Not 'pro-existence', but co-existence.[19] Similarly, Gourdet suggests that identification with the people can only be reached through realistic participation in the life of the people, which requires that we work less *for* the people, and more *with* them.[20]

Without being close to the people we will not be able to develop appropriate ways of communication, because we will not be able to learn from and with them.[21] And learning together with those whom we seek to evangelise is a crucial precondition for any meaningful evangelism.[22] Evangelisation requires an open space in which all participants in the process are welcomed to share their part of the story without limits. Such an open space presupposes a culture of welcome[23], which lays the foundation for trust. Mission requires trust. Marvin Meyers even speaks of a 'question of prior trust' (QPT) ruling all effective Christian[24] mission. Living with the people, joining hands for transformation of life, builds trust and consequently wins people for the Kingdom of God.

Gifted, trained and sent

The mission of God in the world does not just happen – it is a planned and guided enterprise. And the main leader is the Holy Spirit, who is the Lord of mission (2 Corinthians 3:17). The disciples of Jesus were advised by their leader and master not to start their mission until the

---

18 Ibid.
19 Sundermeier 1986:65.
20 Gourdet 1996:407f.
21 Hesselgrave 1991:46.
22 Loewen 1977:36, see also: Gourdet 1996:407; Hiebert 1985:81f.
23 See more about the concept of participation in a culture of welcome in Reimer 2013:140ff.
24 Meyers 1981:32f.

Spirit of God came (Acts 1:8). The coming of the Spirit marked the beginning of the Church and her mission in the world. The Spirit leads the Church in mission, but does so by placing in the Church a wonderful apostolic (missionary) team of apostles, prophets, evangelists, pastors and teachers set to equip the church members to do the ministry to which they have been called (Ephesians 4:11-12).

Apostolic Leadership – led by an apostle.

Apostles determine the missionary vision, character and culture of the Church. Where the Church is led by apostolically gifted people, mission will always be at the heart of the Church.

The Greek term *apostolos* means 'a sent one'. An apostle is a missionary, or a missionary minded, mission-driven leader, who:
- is sent to mission
- understands mission
- is able to strategically organise mission
- teaches the disciples of Christ mission and a missionary vision.

Prophetic Leadership - Prophets are analytically gifted people.

Prophets see into the past, present and future of humans. God reveals to them what hinders and what may promote his mission. They equip the saints by advising them where their placement is (Acts 13:1ff) and when and what is meaningful to do to achieve the best results.

Prophets look into the future and see the potential, and discern the directions and actions for mission to take shape. Without the prophetic leadership mission will degrade to a continuing experiment, never-ending spontaneous action, without any plan and reason. With prophets in leadership the Church will hear God and understand his plan of action. The Church does well not to underestimate und suppress prophecy in her midst. (1 Thessalonians 5:20ff)

Evangelistic Leadership - Evangelists are spirit-gifted communicators of the gospel.

Evangelists lead the church into the public square to engage with the community.

Evangelists know how to bring the message of the Kingdom of God to the people in darkness. They are 'the voice of the Church in the world.' It is the evangelists who teach the Church to communicate the gospel in deed and word meaningfully and effectively. Whenever evangelists are in leadership in the Church, that community of followers will always contextualise their church life, seek ways to speak the language of the people and adapt forms understandable to the people around them.

Pastoral Leadership - Pastors are caregivers of the Church, mission mentors who care for the health and wellbeing of every member.

Pastors are the caretakers of a spiritually and emotionally healthy church.

Pastors correct, reshape and encourage the members of the Church, empowering them for their own mission. Counselling towards a mature missional personality is the aim and task of the pastor. Mission in the world is frontline work. Missionaries going to the mission field will soon experience how dangerous the frontline can become. They will be bruised and will need healing and comfort.

Teacher Leadership - Teachers lay theological foundations of the Church in mission.

Missional churches value the ministry of teachers.

The first church in Jerusalem knew how important solid theology was and, therefore, they met weekly to study the word of God and the teachings of the apostles. (Acts 2:42) The Church should never develop without sound biblical teaching. (1 Timothy 2:2) The danger of false teachings leading to heresy is obvious.

An **apostolic leadership team** is set to equip the saints for ministry and mission. Where such a team is installed the church members will grow spiritually and act missionally (Ephesians 4:13-16). As a result the Church will grow naturally (Ephesians 4:16) in her love for God and the people around them.

Sign and messenger of the Kingdom

THE missional Church proclaims the Gospel of the Kingdom. She prays as Jesus taught: 'Your kingdom come on earth as it is in heaven' and she concentrates on the Kingdom first in everything she does, knowing that God will provide whatever she needs. (Matthew 6:33) She is first and foremost Kingdom-driven, a Kingdom community, and a sign and messenger of the Kingdom of God. The Kingdom orientation of the Church has a number of consequences for any church development on earth:

- **The Church representing God's Kingdom can never be totally at home on earth.** She is an expression of God's Kingdom in everything she is and does. Her form, expressions and programmes must communicate God's idea of life, community and culture.

- **The Church representing God's Kingdom is in principle holistic and integral.** She covers the whole of life. She is interested in spiritual as well as social, political and material matters of life. There can be no dualism between the sacred and secular, the spiritual and the social. In fact, all aspects of life are covered by the interest to transform the socio-cultural space, the *ethnos*, into a disciple of Christ, as the great commission suggests (Matthew 28:19-20).

- **The Church representing God's Kingdom is community-centred.** She is God's *ecclesia*, called out of the world of people to accept responsibility for the world we live in. Community development is what she does in her mission.

- **The Church representing God's Kingdom is intrinsically evangelistic.** She is set to proclaim the Gospel, and she communicates this in life, deeds and words. Evangelism here is an integral process including elements of life-witness, social engagement for a better life, and verbal proclamation.[25]

- **The Church representing God's Kingdom is a sign and example of the new humanity.** The Church is God's people; she represents a matrix of God's idea of a good and righteous life. (2 Corinthians 5:21) In her, God realises his idea of peoplehood with all the elements of establishing a nation. The mission of the Church is discipling nations and teaching them to live according to what Jesus teaches. (Matthew 28:19)

And what a compelling mission that is!

---

[25] See more in Reimer 2013b: 226-246.

Bibliography

BARRETT, Lois. 2006. Defining Missional Church. In: Evangelical, Ecumenical and Anabaptist Missiology in Conversation. Essays in honor of Wilbert R. Shenk, ed. by James R. Krabill, Walter Sawatzky and Charles E. Van Engen. Maryknoll, NY: Orbis, pp. 177-183.

BARTH, Karl. 1962. Church Dogmatics IV/3. Edinburgh: T.&T. Clark.

BETZ, O. 1990. Prophetie", in Das große Bibellexikon. Bd. 3, hrsg. von H. Burkhardt, F. Grünzweig, F. Laubach, G. Meier. Wuppertal und Gießen.

BONHOEFFER, Dietrich. 1971. Letters and Papers from Prison. The enlarged edition. London: SCM Press.

BOSCH, David J. 2011. Transforming Mission. Paradigm Shifts in Theology of Mission. Maryknoll, NY: Orbis.

COENEN, L. 1972. Kirche", in Theologisches Begriffslexikon zum Neuen Testament, hrsg. von L. Coenen, E. Beireuther, H. Biedenhard. 3. Auflage. Wuppertal: Brockhaus.

COSTAS, Orlando E. 1974. The Church and its Mission. A Shattering Critique from the Third World. Wheaton: Tyndale House Publishers.

1982. Christ Outside the Gate. Mission Beyond Christendom. Maryknoll: Orbis.

DAHL, S. 2001. "Einführung in die Interkulturelle Kommunikation". In: http://www.intercultural-network.de/einführung (19.06.2013).

FERRARO, Gary. 1998. Cultural Anthropology: An Applied Perspective. Independence: Wadsworth.

FROST, Michael and Hirsch, Alan. 2003. Shaping of Things to Come.

Innovation and Mission for the 21st Century Church. Peabody: Hendrickson.

GIBBS, Eddy and Bolger, Ryan K. 2005. Emerging Churches. Grand Rapids, MI: Baker.

GIBBS, Eddie and Ryan K. Bolger. 2006. Post Modern Forms of the Church. In Evangelical, Ecumenical and Anabaptist Missiologies in Conversation. Essays in Honor of Wilbert Shenk, ed. By James R. Krabill, Walter Sawatzky and Charles E. Van Engen. Maryknoll: Orbis, pp. 184-195.

GOURDET, S. 1996. Identification in Intercultural Communication. Missionalia 24:3, pp. 399-409.

GRUDEM. Wayne.1988. The Gift of Prophecy in the New Testament and Today. Eastbourne: IVP.

1994. Die Gabe der Prophetie. Nürnberg: VTR.

GUDER, Darrell I. 1998. Missional Church. A Vision for the Sending of the Church in North America. Grand Rapids, MI. Eerdmans.

HESSELGRAVE, David J. Communicating Christ Cross-Culturally. An Introduction to Missionary Communication. Grand Rapids: Zondervan.

HIEBERT, Paul G. 1985. Anthropological Insights for Missionaries. Grand Rapids: Baker.

LOEWEN, Jacob A. 1977. Culture and Human Values: Christian Interpretation in Anthropological Perspective. Pasadena, CA: WCL.

LUTHER, Martin. 1537: Smalcald Articles (III, XII). http://bookofconcord.org/smalcald.php (21.02.2016).

MAYERS, Marvin K 1981. Christianity Confronts Culture. Grand Rapids: Zondervan.

MCGAVRAN, Donald. 1990. Gemeindewachstum verstehen. Eine grundlegende Einführung in die Theologie des Gemeindeaufbaus. Lörrach: Simson.

MCNEAL, Reggie. 2009. Missional Renaissance. Changing the Scorecard for the Church. San Francisco: Jossey-Bass.

MOLTMANN, Jürgen.1975. Kirche in der Kraft des Geistes. München: Kaiser.

1967. Theology of Hope: On the Ground and the Implications of a Christian Eschatology, London: SCM Press.

PADILLA, René . 1985. Mission Between the Times. Essays on the Kingdom. Grand Rapids: Eerdmans.

REIMER, Johannes. 2013. Die Welt umarmen. Theologie des gesellschaftsrelevanten Gemeindebaus. Transformationsstudien Bd. 1. 2. Auflage. Marburg: Francke Verlag.

2013a. Leben. Rufen. Verändern. Chancen und Herausforderungen gesellschaftsrelevanter Evangelisation heute. Marburg: Francke Verlag.

2013b. Hereinspaziert. Willkommenskultur und Evangelisation. Schwarzenfeld: Neufeld.

ROXBURGH, Alan J. 1997. Missionary Congregation, Leadership & Liminality. Harrisburg: Trinity Press International.

SCHWEIZER, Eduard. 1959. Gemeinde und Gemeindeordnung im Neuen Testament. Zürich: Zwingli Verlag.

SHENCK, Wilbert R. 1983. Exploring Church Growth. Grand Rapids: Eerdmans.

SUNDERMEIER, Theo. 1986. Konvivenz als Grundstruktur ökumenischer Existenz heute. In: Ökumenische Existenz Heute 1, pp 49-100.

WARREN, Rick. 1998. Kirche mit Vision: Gemeinde die den Auftrag lebt. Asslar: Projektion J.

ZUNKEL, C. Wayne. 1987. Church Growth under Fire. Kitchener: Herald Press.

Micah Global is a world-wide movement of Christian organisations, institutions and individuals networking and acting together towards a transforming and integral mission that sees the church as an agent of change in every community.

We are a catalyst, a movement and a network for transforming mission with a special focus on mobilising a united response towards reducing poverty, addressing injustice and enabling reconciliation and conflict resolution around the world.

We work to deepen the understanding and application of integral mission as expressed through ministry responses such as relief, rehabilitation, development, creation care, justice, and peace-making and reconciliation initiatives.

Established in 2001, Micah now has over 800 members in 93 countries. Our vision inspires us towards the realisation of communities living life in all its fullness, free from extreme poverty, injustice or conflict.

> Micah Global's motivating call to action is expressed in Micah 6:8. "What does the Lord require of you? To act justly and to love mercy, and to walk humbly with your God."

Connect with us www.micahglobal.org

Lightning Source UK Ltd.
Milton Keynes UK
UKHW02f1254081018
330187UK00003B/98/P